KINGFISHER LANDM

Wolfgang Amadeus
MOZART

ALAN KENDALL

Kingfisher Books

Contents

Introduction

The year 1991 commemorates the two-hundredth anniversary of the death of Mozart. He died in poverty, in his thirty-sixth year, and yet today he is one of the most famous and most admired composers that ever lived.

Mozart was a child prodigy. He made his first public appearance as a keyboard player and wrote his first music at the age of five. From then on until his death he poured out a remarkable succession of masterpieces – operas, masses, symphonies, concertos and chamber music – most of which have survived and are still performed today.

The 18th century – the time at which Mozart was composing – is often thought of as the 'Age of Classicism': a period of strict control of form and proportion in art and architecture, music and literature. Mozart's music is seen to be a product of this age. At the same time, it has a depth of feeling and power of expression that look ahead to the music of a new age that was to come. We call this new age the 'Age of Romanticism'.

This is what makes Mozart such an important landmark in the history of music. His work appeals to a great variety of people throughout the world.

The Mozart family at home.

Mozart's World

In Mozart's time, even more than today, musicians accepted the need to travel in search of work. Mozart himself covered an enormous area of Europe, from Naples to Berlin and from Prague to London. He began his travels as a six-year-old child prodigy, and made his last journey only weeks before his death. In the course of his various travels he met many of the royal families of Europe. Sadly, though, those who had been happy to make a fuss of the child prodigy were reluctant to help the penniless and apparently unsuccessful mature composer. Constant travelling as a child may have contributed to the restless, improvident disorder that marked his adult life.

SCOTLAND

Scott 1771–1832
(Novelist and poet)
● Edinburgh
Burns 1759–96
(Poet)

IRELAND

● Dublin

NORTH SEA

ENGLAND

Johnson 1709–84
(Critic)

WALES

Paine 1737–1809
(Philosopher)

NETHERLA...

● Amste...

Reynolds
1723–92
(Painter)

● London

● Brussels

Flaxman 1755–1826
(Sculptor)

● Lille

Cologne

Turner 1775–1851
(Painter)

Lamarck 1744–1829 Bon...
(Naturalist)

Beetho...
1770–1...
(Compo...

Blake 1757–1827
(Poet and painter)

Rouen

Seine

● Paris

Fragonard
1732–1806
(Painter)

David 1748–
1825 (Painter)

Strasbo...

Diderot 1713–84
(Philosopher and writer)

Loire

Voltaire 1694–1778
(Philosopher and writer)

FRANCE

SWITZERLA...

Geneva ●

AL...

Lyons ●

Rousse...
1712–78
(Philoso...
and write...

● Bordeaux

Garonne

Rhône

Ge...

Ebro

Douro

● Marseilles

PORTUGAL

PYRENEES

**Napoleon
Bonaparte**
1769–1821
(Emperor o...
the French)...

Tagus

SPAIN

● Zaragoza

Lisbon ●

● Madrid

Goya 1746–1828
(Painter)

● Barcelona

Guadiana

● Seville

MEDITERRANEAN SEA

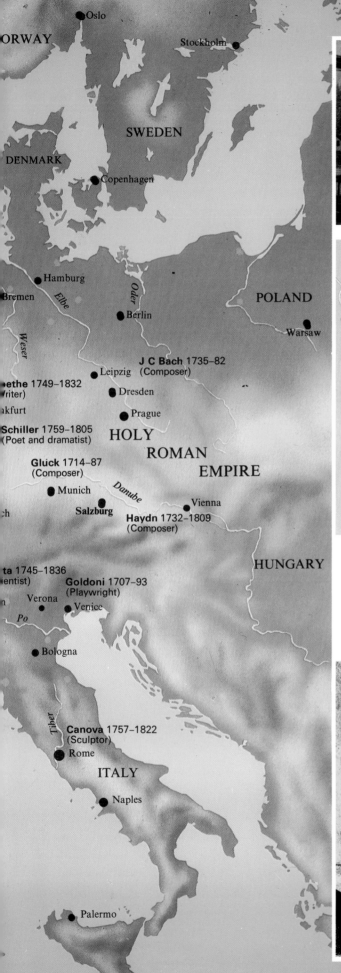

Oslo

NORWAY

Stockholm

SWEDEN

DENMARK

Copenhagen

Hamburg

Bremen

Elbe

Oder

POLAND

Weser

Berlin

Warsaw

J C Bach 1735–82
(Composer)

Leipzig

Goethe 1749–1832
(Writer)

Dresden

Frankfurt

Prague

Schiller 1759–1805
(Poet and dramatist)

HOLY
ROMAN
EMPIRE

Gluck 1714–87
(Composer)

Danube

Munich

Vienna

Salzburg

Haydn 1732–1809
(Composer)

HUNGARY

...ta 1745–1836
(...entist)

Goldoni 1707–93
(Playwright)

Verona

Venice

Po

Bologna

Tiber

Canova 1757–1822
(Sculptor)

Rome

ITALY

Naples

Palermo

St Petersburg
(Leningrad)

RUSSIA

Berlin

Weser

Oder

Elbe

Cologne
Bonn

Kassel

Leipzig

Weimar

Dresden

Koblenz

Frankfurt

Mainz

Mannheim

Heidelberg

Nuremberg

Prague

Rhine

Stuttgart

Danube

Augsburg

Munich

Linz

VIENNA
Mödling
Baden

Salzburg

THE ALPS

*Above: During the 18th
century, Germany was a
loose federation of more
than 400 states. All owed
a nominal allegiance to
the Holy Roman Emperor,
whose seat was in Vienna.*

*Top: A contemporary view
of Mannheim, a great
musical centre.
Below: Mozart's birth-
place, then No. 225,
Löchelplatz, Salzburg. It
was an elegant address.*

7

Early Years

Wolfgang Amadeus Mozart was born in the beautiful city of Salzburg on January 27th, 1756. Today, Salzburg is in Austria, just across the border from Germany. But at that time, Salzburg was a small, independent state ruled by its own prince-archbishop. It was noted for its Baroque cathedral, its University and had a fine reputation for music and the arts.

Mozart's father, Leopold, was a professional musician who played in the Court orchestra. Over the years he rose to become Court Composer and Assistant Kapellmeister (music director) to the then prince-archbishop, Sigismund Christoph von Schrattenbach. He was respected both as a composer and as a teacher, and was the author of a famous textbook on violin playing. In 1747 Leopold married Anna Maria Pertl. In all, the couple were to have seven children – but only Wolfgang and his elder sister, Maria Anna, survived.

Below: A view of the city of Salzburg, with its baroque cathedral (centre), dominated by the medieval palace (right) of the prince-archbishops.

Right: The seven-year-old Mozart, with Leopold and Maria Anna ('Nannerl'). Brother and sister gave many concerts together between 1762 and 1766.

Maria Anna – 'Nannerl' to the family – was four and a half years older than her brother. She was highly musical, and had the benefit of her father's first-rate teaching. By the age of eight she was already a fine keyboard player. But from early on, Wolfgang began to show quite outstanding musical gifts. At three he eagerly joined in Nannerl's music lessons with her father. He had a wonderful memory for melody and harmony and a miraculous talent for the piano. At the age of four he was discovered with a sheet of paper covered with inky scribbles. He announced to his astonished father that he was writing a concerto – and proved it by sitting down to play what he had just written!

Convinced that he had a genius on his hands, Leopold set aside his own ambitions and devoted himself entirely to his son's education. We can still read Leopold's excited comments on Wolfgang's progress. There seemed to be no limits to what the boy could do. But how was his child prodigy to be introduced to the world?

Leopold decided to take his musical children on a tour of the aristocratic courts of Europe. It was quite common at the time for gifted children to be paraded before aristocratic audiences – almost like circus turns. Naturally the adults who managed them hoped for financial reward. But we should not think of Leopold as an exploiter. He was a devoted husband and father. But he received only a small salary from his position at Court – and he felt a responsibility to do the best he could for his family.

Some musical instruments of Mozart's time. Top to bottom: viola d'amore, oboe, flute and French horn. The 'sound' of such instruments was often softer than modern versions.

Two Tours

In 1762, Leopold took his brilliant children on their first concert tour. Wolfgang was only six years old. They visited the nearby German city of Munich, then travelled on to Vienna, capital of the Holy Roman Empire. There Wolfgang and Nannerl played before the Empress Maria-Theresa and her six-year-old daughter Marie-Antoinette – later to become the ill-fated Queen of France. The Empress made a great fuss of Wolfgang – she gave him and his sister magnificent outfits for their appearances at court.

After his triumph in Vienna, Leopold returned to Salzburg. He was now planning a much more ambitious tour to take in Germany, the Netherlands, France and England. The family left Salzburg in June 1763 and did not return until November 1766. In both Paris and London the Mozarts played before the royal family as well as giving public concerts. Wolfgang also met composers like Johann Schobert (1720–67) and Johann Christian Bach (1735–82) who did much to encourage and influence his music.

Above: Young Mozart plays the harpsichord before an aristocratic tea-party at the house of the French Prince de Conti. From a painting by the artist Ollivier.

Above: Wolfgang in the gold-braided violet gala dress given to him in Vienna in 1762 by the Empress Maria-Theresa. Leopold had him painted in it as a souvenir. Nannerl received a dress of white silk.

10

Life on the Road

Travel in the 18th century was an uncomfortable and costly business. Established mail- and passenger-coach routes linked main centres. But an average day's travel barely covered 50 kilometres, and it was necessary to make overnight stops at wayside inns. Broken axles, overturned coaches, surly coachmen and bug-ridden inns were commonplace. In the winter things were even worse, with the roads deep in mud and long delays at seaports waiting for ships to put to sea. To avoid the worst, the Mozart family travelled in summer, visiting the grand houses of the nobility along the way. Noble families, in the country for the summer, were usually glad of the entertainment provided by Wolfgang and Nannerl. Along the route the Mozarts also stopped at towns and cities. In Frankfurt, for instance, the great German writer Goethe, then fourteen, heard the seven-year-old Mozart play. He remembered especially the powdered wig and sword that Wolfgang wore. The crossing to England in 1764 was particularly uncomfortable. The regular packet-boat was full and the Mozarts had to take a smaller ship – and they were sea-sick as a result.

Left: In London, Mozart wrote a setting of the psalm, God is Our Refuge, which he gave to the new British Museum. He wrote it in what he imagined to be the 'ancient style' of English church music.

Below: A view of London in 1749, looking much as it must have done in Mozart's day. London's river frontage, dominated by St Paul's, was renowned as one of the most beautiful in Europe.

Arts of the Mid-18th Century

Above: The Swing, *by the French painter Jean-Honoré Fragonard (1732–1806). It was painted in 1766. In pictures like these, Fragonard effortlessly captured the 18th century aristocratic taste for frivolous gallantry.*

During the mid-18th century, important changes happened in painting, sculpture and literature. You can get some idea of the shift that took place by comparing the picture on the left with the two pictures on the far right. There was a deliberate turning away from a decorative lightness and gallantry to a more solemn and serious approach. The new art began in Rome and drew on the ideas of ancient Greek and ancient Roman art. It was given added weight by the discoveries made at Herculaneum and Pompeii over the period 1738 to 1756. This interest in ancient sources gave the movement its name – Classicism. But it was more than a mere fashion: the leaders of the movement truly believed that ancient art held a high seriousness that they should try to copy in their own work. Classicism in art emphasised order, reason and the 'noble simplicities' of the ancient world. It attacked ornament and decoration as 'unnatural'. In much the same way, writers and thinkers were beginning to attack the powers wielded by selfish, privileged monarchs and aristocrats.

Mozart's Musical World

Classicism in music is much harder to isolate than in the visual arts. More than any other art form of this period, music was most closely wedded to the social system. Musicians depended on rich patrons for employment. And as Mozart found to his cost, without a patron it was impossible to make a living. The patron who paid the salary was also able to call the tune. As a result, most music was professional, craftsmanlike, but conventional, reflecting the conservative tastes of aristocratic patrons. Even in the expanding world of commercial opera houses and public concerts things were little better. Public taste was fickle and composers had to be highly adaptable to survive. In the absence of copyright laws, composers rarely made money from their music once it was published. Such conditions made it difficult for Mozart to work as a freelance – although his innate genius created great music in spite of them. Only with Beethoven do we enter a period when composers in general gained full artistic freedom.

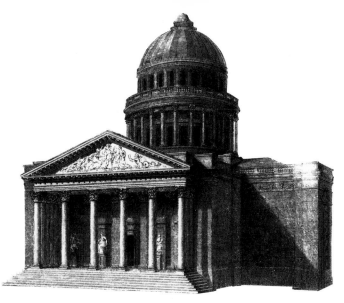

Right: The Panthéon, Paris, built in the years after 1755. The typically Classical design was based on the Pantheon in Rome, completed AD 120.

Left: The German operatic composer Christoph Gluck (1714–87). His immensely successful operas were based on ancient Greek stories.

Below left: Joseph Haydn (1732–1809) was lucky to find a generous patron. Unlike Mozart, he never knew hardship.

Left: The Oath of the Horatii (1784) by David (1748–1825). Its severity contrasts sharply with the lightness of The Swing (page 14).

Below: 18th-century 'Chamber Music' was written to be performed in the salons (chambers) of wealthy aristocrats.

Italian Interlude

The great European tour of 1763 to 1766 was terribly hard work. Leopold, Nannerl and Wolfgang were all seriously ill at one time or another. But the tour was a great success. The Mozarts gained an international reputation. Just as important, young Wolfgang was able to meet, and learn from, the best musicians and composers of the day. He quickly mastered the different musical styles that he encountered.

In London, Italianate music and Italian opera were immensely fashionable. Johann Christian Bach, the composer who became the Mozarts' great friend, had studied in Italy. Bach and his circle convinced Leopold that he should complete Wolfgang's musical education by taking him to Italy – the source of the most exciting musical developments of the time. This plan, however, took three years to come about. After England, the tour ground on for more than a year. Then there was a nine-month break in Salzburg before Leopold took the family off to Vienna.

The Mozarts spent a troubled year in Vienna. Wolfgang and Nannerl caught smallpox in an epidemic which virtually closed down the city. There were few concerts. Mozart wrote two operas, *Bastien und Bastienne*, and another *La finta semplice* – commissioned by the new Emperor, Josef II. But Leopold could not get them performed publicly in Vienna. The Mozarts returned to Salzburg.

Above: Public transport in Italy was primitive. This type of mule-drawn carriage was called a venturino. The Mozarts could afford to travel by private carriage. But they were still in fear of attacks by bandits on the road from Naples to Rome.

Left: Hieronymus Colloredo (1732–1812), the last Prince-Archbishop of Salzburg. Despite Mozart's musical tribute to him when he took office, the new archbishop made life more and more difficult for the young composer. Finally Mozart left his service.

Left: Wolfgang at the age of twenty-one. From 1772 to 1777 he found it difficult to escape from Salzburg. Unlike Schrattenbach, Colloredo expected his employees to do what they were paid to do. Leave of absence was only grudgingly granted.

The time was now ripe for the planned trip to Italy. In December 1769, father and son set off, leaving Nannerl at home with her mother. Their tour was a triumphal progress through all the major Italian cities, from Milan and Florence to Naples, Rome and back. The city of Milan commissioned Mozart to write an opera, *Mitridate* ('King Mithridates'). He conducted its first performance on December 26th, 1770, to a tremendous reception. In Rome, the Pope made him a Knight of the Golden Spur. More honours and commissions followed.

In the midst of these triumphs, Archbishop Schrattenbach died, to be succeeded by an Italian, Hieronymus Colloredo. No one could then foresee what a blow this would turn out to be. Mozart, still busy fulfilling his Italian commissions, wrote a *serenata* in honour of his new master. Entitled *Il Sogno di Scipione* (Scipio's Dream'), it was performed at the beginning of May, 1772. In October the Mozarts set off again for Italy, for the première of a new opera, *Lucio Silla*, in Milan.

Above: Keepsakes given to Mozart on his Italian tour by rulers and dignitaries. On their first long tour, Leopold complained that gifts were no substitute for hard cash needed to hire halls, pay musicians and keep his family in suitable style.

Below: Piranesi's view of the Pantheon in Rome. During his stay, Mozart heard Allegri's jealously-guarded Miserere *in the Sistine Chapel and transcribed the piece from memory.*

Hard Times: Mannheim and Paris

The Mozarts found that Archbishop Colloredo was a very different character from the easy-going Schrattenbach. In his eyes composers were just like any other of his servants. They were there to do what he asked them to. He kept Mozart hard at work in Salzburg. Although Mozart received many requests for new music outside Salzburg, Colloredo refused to grant father and son leave of absence for their travels. It seemed that the only solution was for Wolfgang to resign his post and find a position abroad, while Leopold remained at home to earn a living for his family.

In 1777 Colloredo was persuaded to dismiss Mozart as Assistant Konzertmeister. With his

Right: The young Aloysia Weber, with whom Mozart fell in love when he was twenty-one. At that time Aloysia was only fifteen. She later married the actor and painter Josef Lange.

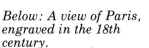

Below: A view of Paris, engraved in the 18th century.

Below: The market square of the city of Mannheim, as it may have looked to Mozart. Mannheim, on the river Rhine, was called the Athens of Germany. Its fine reputation for art and culture was the work of its ruler, the Elector Karl Theodor. He deliberately set out to rival the architecture and brilliant court life of the French royal palace at Versailles. Karl Theodor's orchestra, founded by Johann Stammitz (1717–57) was the most famous in Germany. In Mannheim, Mozart made many friends among the community of Austrian and Bohemian musicians.

Above: This portrait of Mozart's mother is part of a larger painting of the Mozart family completed by Croce in 1781.

Below: Mozart playing to a group of friends. The company of fellow musicians in Mannheim was of great value to him.

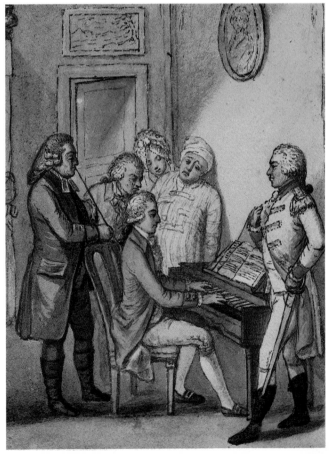

mother as travelling companion, Wolfgang began a tour to Mannheim via Munich and Augsburg. In those days the orchestra at Mannheim was the most famous in Europe. Contact with it was an important stage in Mozart's career. Even so there was no prospect of the appointment that Mozart so badly needed. The next thought was to try Paris. With luck he could earn his living there – even without an appointment.

Leopold gave his approval. But Wolfgang lingered in Mannheim. He had fallen in love with a young singer called Aloysia Weber, the daughter of a court musician. Anxiously, Leopold wrote letters pointing out that until Wolfgang had made his way in the world, he could not possibly think of marriage. Finally, in March 1778, Wolfgang and his mother left Mannheim for Paris.

In Paris, however, Wolfgang fared little better. Nobody took any notice of his operas. And Mozart seemed to have no idea how to make a career for himself. Then disaster struck. His mother fell ill, and in July she died. He left Paris for home, via Mannheim and Munich, where he visited Aloysia Weber. But Aloysia seemed no longer to care for him. Mozart was forced back to Salzburg, to take up the post of Court Organist.

Life in Vienna

Although Mozart did not greatly enjoy the next two years in Salzburg, he wrote a great deal of music. He composed two Masses for the cathedral choir there, three new symphonies for the court orchestra and a great masterpiece, the *Sinfonia Concertante* for violin and viola. Then, in the autumn of 1780, he was commissioned by the Court at Munich to write an opera, *Idomeneo*. Courtesy demanded that Colloredo release him. He left for Munich on November 5th, and the first performance on January 29th, 1781, was an immediate success. It seemed that after this an appointment must surely come. Mozart hung on hopefully in Munich, but nothing was offered.

Meanwhile Colloredo was in Vienna, angry with Mozart for outstaying his leave, but pleased to have such a famous musician in his service. On the 12th of March, he summoned Mozart to Vienna. Mozart could not refuse, but determined to be free of the Archbishop as soon as possible. After a campaign of deliberate impertinence, Mozart was literally kicked out of the Archbishop's residence on the 8th of June.

Below: Between 1770 and 1790 Vienna grew into a great centre of music, literature and the arts. The Emperor Josef II encouraged the growth of a wealthy, educated and cultured middle class. Such people were forward-looking and eager for new ideas, especially in the arts. In this atmosphere, Mozart found, for a time, true recognition – if not always financial rewards.

Above: Mozart's wife Constanze, in a portrait by her brother-in-law Josef Lange. Leopold suspected her mother of trapping Wolfgang into marriage. Nannerl thought that Constanze was a most unsuitable wife for her brother. But all evidence shows that Wolfgang was devoted to his wife and that the marriage was happy.

Mozart moved in with his old Mannheim friends, the Webers, who were now in Vienna. He was convinced that his high reputation among the Viennese aristocracy would provide him with pupils, commissions and a ready audience for his concerts. Almost immediately the Emperor commissioned him to write a German opera. The result, *Die Entführung aus dem Serail* ('The Abduction from the Seraglio'), had its first performance on July 16th, 1782. It was another success, and it seemed that the tide had truly turned for Mozart when, on August 4th, he married Constanze Weber, the younger sister of his first love, Aloysia.

Above: A ticket for one of the many concerts that Mozart gave in Vienna.

Right: The Burgtheater (extreme right) was the scene of Vienna's most glittering musical occasions.

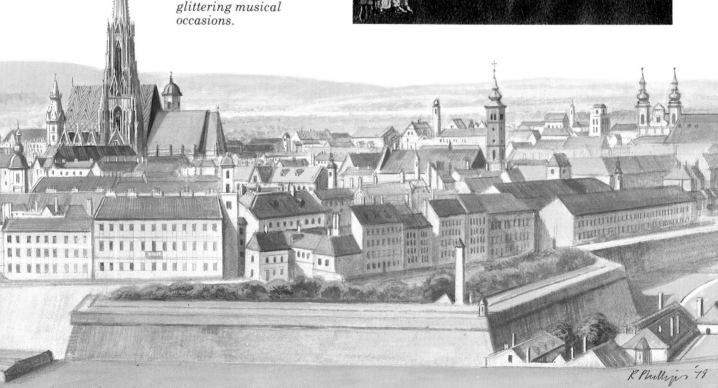

Mozart the Dramatist

Mozart was fascinated by opera from the age of eight. By the time he was twenty-five he had already written thirteen operas. Most were in the Italian 'number-opera' style, fashionable for most of the 18th century. They were slow-moving, extravagant, spectacular showpieces for individual singers. The action repeatedly stopped for 'numbers' – solos, duets, trios which might last for ten minutes or more, to be followed by applause, encores, bows and bouquets. No wonder that the first performance of Mozart's *Mitridate* lasted for six hours.

After settling in Vienna, however, Mozart began to develop entirely new forms of opera combining music, drama, singing and acting in an unbroken, natural and harmonious movement. The plots of these operas are affected by the anti-aristocratic, anti-Catholic atmosphere of Josef II's Vienna and pre-Revolutionary France. The first of them, *The Marriage of Figaro* (1786), is a brilliant comedy about a selfish aristocrat who is outwitted by his servants.

Above: Joseph Quaglio's set for the 1793 Munich production of The Magic Flute, *written in the last year of Mozart's life. The plot is a strange mixture of comedy, farce, fantasy and religious ritual. At its highest level it is about human brotherhood, the ideal of the Freemasons, to whom Mozart belonged.*

Left: Papageno, the comic bird-catcher from The Magic Flute. *In the original production the part was played by the actor, singer and impresario Emanuel Schikaneder, who also wrote the libretto. This illustration is from the 1816 Berlin production.*

Below: Pamina, the heroine of The Magic Flute. *She falls in love with an Egyptian prince, Tamino.*

Four Great Operas

Mozart read through hundreds of plays and stories in search of a plot for his first new-style opera. *Figaro* was based on a comedy by the radical French dramatist Beaumarchais (1732–99). The text (libretto) was written by an Italian poet, former priest and likeable rogue, Lorenzo Da Ponte. Mozart took immense pains with every aspect of producing the opera. He knew that it would make great demands on his singers, who would have to carry along the action at every moment by song, speech and gesture. In all, Mozart's collaboration with Da Ponte produced three operas, *Figaro* (1786), *Don Giovanni* (1787) and *Così fan tutte* (1790). In them Mozart enabled opera, for the first time, to express the emotions and character in a convincing, natural-seeming way. In the last year of his life, Mozart made another radical departure with *The Magic Flute* (1791). Here Mozart totally transformed a frothy entertainment originally dreamt up by his fellow-Freemason Emanuel Schikaneder. Somehow Mozart's music was able to bring together elements of pantomime, comedy and fantasy with the most serious reflections on life, death and Masonic ideals of brotherhood.

Top: Emanuel Schikaneder.
Above: Lorenzo Da Ponte, librettist of The Marriage of Figaro, Don Giovanni *and* Così fan tutte.

Below Right: The title-page of music arranged from an early edition of Così fan tutte.
Below: Luigi Bassi, the first Don Giovanni.

Triumph and Tragedy

The last ten years of Mozart's life were based in Vienna. At last he was free to live his own life, away from the demands of a master. And by marrying Constanze, he removed himself somewhat from his father's influence. Independence and the stimulating atmosphere of Vienna, bore fruit in some of his greatest works.

Mozart's new life was a torrent of activity. There were concerts, lessons and payments from music publishers. He seemed set for a dazzling career. He composed prolifically, including the first two of six string quartets dedicated to Haydn.

In the summer of 1783, Wolfgang felt confident enough to visit Leopold in Salzburg. Leopold was finally convinced that his son's prospects were bright. But he was still worried about Wolfgang's lack of business sense. Two years later the old man visited the Mozarts in Vienna, where he was at first dazzled but later exhausted by the hectic pace of life. But he had the pleasure of hearing Haydn praising his son's great genius.

The triumph of *The Marriage of Figaro* was followed up by a commission to write a new opera, *Don Giovanni* (1787). A third opera, *Così fan tutte* was written in 1790, while *The Magic Flute* and *La Clemenza di Tito* were written in the last year of his life. During all this time a constant stream of other compositions flowed from his pen.

In 1787 Leopold died. The same year Mozart was made Court Composer to the Emperor at a substantial salary. But despite apparent successes, Mozart was desperately short of funds. His pride demanded that he keep up appearances: few of his friends realized that he was deeply in debt.

Had his health held up he would probably have got over the crisis. He made two tours, one to Berlin and one to Frankfurt, but travelling expenses took most of the money. A kidney disease was meanwhile sapping his strength. In 1791 he worked furiously on the two operas and a Requiem Mass. But his illness got worse and on December 5th he died. He was buried in an unmarked grave.

Below: Mozart plays the quartets that he dedicated to Haydn. The listeners are Haydn himself, Leopold (seated) and Constanze. The recital took place in Mozart's house in 1785. Haydn told Leopold: 'Before God, I tell you as an honest man that your son is the greatest composer I know in person or by name'.

Left: Prague was the capital of Bohemia, and Mozart had good friends there. Two of his operas, Don Giovanni and La Clemenza di Tito, were first performed at the city's main theatre.

Right: Josef Lange's unfinished portrait of Mozart, painted in the winter of 1789/90.

Below: Mozart's two sons, Karl and Franz Xaver. Although their father was one of the greatest of geniuses, they inherited none of it.

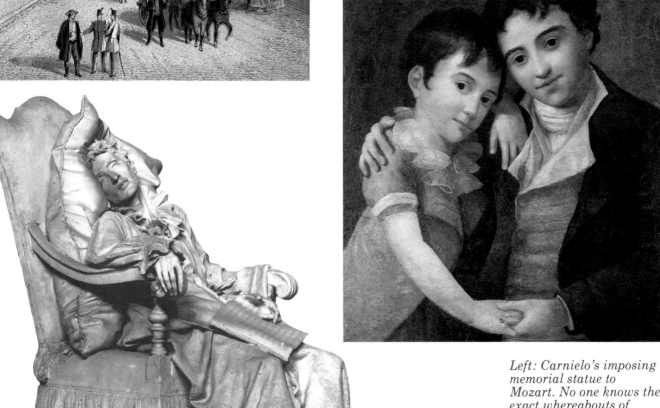

Left: Carnielo's imposing memorial statue to Mozart. No one knows the exact whereabouts of Mozart's grave in the cemetery of St Marx, Vienna. But as long as his music is played, the 'little great man' will have a living memorial.

Part of the set design by Simon Quaglio for a production of The Magic Flute in Munich in 1818. It shows the Temple of the Sun in Egypt, where the opera is set. The Magic Flute was Mozart's last opera, and many people think it is his greatest.

Time Chart

Year	Mozart's Life	Other Events
1756	Born Salzburg, January 27.	War between France and Britain over North American territories.
1757		Birth of Alexander Hamilton, American statesman, and William Blake, English artist and poet; Battle of Plassey – British gain control of Bengal.
1759		French defeated at sea and lose Canada to the British; British Museum opened; Birth of Friedrich Schiller, German writer, and William Pitt the Younger, English statesman; Death of Handel.
1760		Birth of Camille Desmoulins, French revolutionary.
1761	First compositions, Andante and allegro for solo keyboard (written down by father).	
1762	Journey to Munich and Vienna.	Rousseau's *Emile* and *Contrat social*; Birth of Constanze Weber (Mozart's future wife).
1763	Journey to Paris and London (until 1766); Meets Schobert in Paris and J C Bach in London.	
1764	Publication of first printed works: Arrival in London; First symphonies.	British defeat Emperor of Delhi and obtain control of Bengal, Bihar and Orissa; Stamp Tax imposed in American colonies; Spinning jenny invented by Richard Hargreaves; Stanislas Poniatowski placed on throne of Poland by Catherine the Great of Russia.
1765	Concerts in Netherlands.	Robert Clive begins reforms in India; Joseph II Holy Roman Emperor.
1766	Return to Salzburg.	
1767	Journey to Vienna.	
1768	His first commissioned opera, *La finta semplice*; The *singspiel, Bastien und Bastienne*, performed privately in Vienna; Composes a Mass and several symphonies.	
1769	Return to Salzburg; Appointed Konzertmeister to archbishop in November; December 13 leaves for Italy.	Watt's steam engine (perfected 1775).
1770	Composes first string quartet; Hears Allegri's *Miserere* in the Sistine Chapel in Rome and writes it out from memory; Is made a Knight of the Golden Spur by Pope Clement XIV; December 26, first performance of *Mitridate* in Milan.	Birth of Beethoven, William Wordsworth and Georg Hegel; James Cook discovers Botany Bay.
1771	Return to Salzburg at end of March, but in Italy again from August to mid-December; Death of Archbishop Schrattenbach.	
1772	Hieronymus Colloredo appointed archbishop; Mozart writes serenata *Il Sogno di Scipione* in his honour; October 24, leaves once again for Italy; December 26, new opera *Lucio Silla* performed in Milan.	Gustavus III's coup d'état and reforms in Sweden; First partition of Poland by Russia, Prussia and Austria.
1773	March 13, returns to Salzburg, having composed six string quartets and the motet *Exsultate, jubilate*; Visit to Vienna, July–October; Is received by Empress Maria Theresa.	Pope Clement XIV dissolves the Jesuit Order (until 1814).
1774	December 6, journey to Munich.	Louis XVI King of France.
1775	January 13, first performance of *La finta giardiniera* in Munich; March 6 return to Salzburg; April 23, *Il Rè Pastore* performed in Salzburg.	American Revolution (until 1783); Birth of J M Turner, English painter, Jane Austen, and André Ampère, French physicist; Jenner pioneers vaccination.

1776	Resident in Salzburg.	American Declaration of Independence; Adam Smith, economist, publishes his *Wealth of Nations*; Birth of Constable.
1777	September 23, leaves with his mother for Mannheim, via Munich and Augsburg, having resigned from archbishop's service; In Mannheim from October 30 to March 14, 1778; Makes contact with J C Cannabich, director of orchestra; Love affair with Aloysia Weber (though Mozart was eventually to marry her sister, Constanze).	Bushnell invents the torpedo.
1778	Arrival in Paris March 23; Mother's illness and death, July 3; Mozart leaves Paris for Munich September 26; Break with Aloysia; Ballet *Les petits riens* (composed in Paris) first performed this year.	War of Bavarian Succession (to 1779); Opening of La Scala opera house, Milan; Death of Rousseau and Voltaire.
1779	Return to Salzburg mid-January; Appointed Court Organist; Completes Coronation Mass.	James Cook murdered in Hawaii; Spain declares war on Britain (to 1783).
1780	*Idomeneo* commissioned for Munich; Leaves for Munich November 5; Death of Empress Maria Theresa.	
1781	First performance of *Idomeneo* January 29; March 12, summoned to Vienna by archbishop; May 9, resigns; June 8, 'kicked out'; July 30, given libretto for *Die Entführung aus dem Serail*.	Herschel discovers Uranus; Construction of Siberian highway begun.
1782	July 16 first performance of *Die Entführung*; August 4 marriage to Constanze Weber.	Birth of Paganini; Death of J C Bach.
1783	Visit to Leopold in Salzburg by Wolfgang and Constanze; November 4, *Linz* symphony performed; Birth and death of first son, Raimund.	First successful hot-air balloon; Peace of Versailles ends war between America and Britain; Famine in Japan.
1784	Mozart joins Freemasons; Begins catalogue of own works; Birth of son Karl Thomas (died 1856).	Pitt's India Act (government control of political affairs in India); Death of Dr Johnson.
1785	Leopold visits Vienna; End of October, Mozart begins work on *Le Nozze di Figaro*.	
1786	February 7, first performance of *Der Schauspiel-direktor*; First performance of *Figaro* May 1; Birth and death of son Johann Thomas Leopold.	Death of Frederick II of Prussia; Birth of Weber.
1787	Journey to Prague in January for first performance there of *Figaro*; *Prague* symphony performed and contract signed for *Don Giovanni*; February return to Vienna; May death of Leopold; Beethoven in Vienna; Return to Prague for first performance of *Don Giovanni* on October 29; December 7, appointed Composer to the Imperial Chamber in succession to Gluck; Birth of a daughter, Therese.	American Constitution signed; Death of Gluck; Wilkinson's iron-hull ship built.
1788	May 7 first performance of *Don Giovanni* in Vienna; During summer three symphonies written but probably not performed; Death of daughter.	First convicts transported from Britain to Australia; Birth of Byron.
1789	Journey to Prague, Dresden, Leipzig and Berlin, April 8 to June 4; Clarinet quintet; Composition of *Così fan tutte* begun at end of year; Birth and death of daughter Anna on 16 November.	Beginning of French Revolution; George Washington made first President of United States.
1790	January 27 first performance of *Così fan tutte*; Coronation of Leopold II on death of Emperor Joseph II. Süssmayr (who completed the *Requiem*) becomes Mozart's pupil.	
1791	March meeting with Schikaneder for *Magic Flute*; May 9, appointed unpaid assistant Kapellmeister at St Stephen's, Vienna; July, *Requiem* commissioned by Count Walsegg zu Stuppach; September 6. *La Clemenza di Tito* given first performance in Prague; September 30. *Magic Flute* given first performance in Vienna; Birth of son Franz Xaver Wolfgang (died 1844); Completes Clarinet Concerto; Death of Mozart December 5.	Bill of Rights (first ten amendments to American Constitution).

Mozart's Greatest Works

In the following list, works are usually followed by the letter K. and a number. Although Mozart began to catalogue his works in 1784, it was the Austrian geologist and botanist, Dr Ludwig Ritter von Köchel (1800–1877), who drew up the first comprehensive catalogue of the composer's works. These bear the letter K. for Köchel, and then the number. This numbering has had to be revised in places as our knowledge of the chronology of Mozart's music has become more accurate, but Köchel's system is still basically the same one that we use today.

VOCAL MUSIC

Mozart's father was in the service of the Church in Salzburg, and it was expected that the son would follow in the same tradition and gain a position similar to his father's. Vocal music was always important to Mozart, but he soon discovered that it was in the theatre, rather than the Church, that he felt most at home.

Operas: *Idomeneo*, K. 366 (1781); *Die Entführung aus dem Serail*, K. 384 (1782); *The Marriage of Figaro*, K. 492 (1786); *Don Giovanni*, K. 527 (1787); *Così fan tutte*, K. 588 (1790); *La Clemenza di Tito*, K. 621 (1791); *The Magic Flute*, K. 620 (1791).

Masses and church music: *Exsultate, jubilate*, K. 165 (1773); *Coronation* Mass, K. 317 (1779); Vespers, K. 339 (1780) C minor Mass, K. 427 (1783); *Ave verum corpus*, K. 618 (1791); Requiem Mass, K. 626 (1791).

ORCHESTRAL MUSIC

Mozart would almost certainly have written more symphonies, had he lived, for in the last one he was on the threshold of new developments. His piano concertos were often written for his own performance, whereas the other concertos tended to be written in response to other gifted performers with whom he came into contact.

Symphonies: No. 25 in G minor, K. 183 (1773); No. 29 in A, K. 201 (1774); No. 31 in D, K. 297 (1778) *Paris*; No. 32 in G, K. 318 (1779); No. 33 in B flat, K. 319 (1779); No. 34 in C, K. 338 (1780); No. 35 in D, K. 385 (1782) *Haffner*; No. 36 in C, K. 425 (1783) *Linz*; No. 38 in D, K. 504 (1786) *Prague*; No. 39 in E flat, K. 543 (1788); No. 40 in G minor, K. 550 (1788); No. 41 in C, K. 551 (1788) *Jupiter*; Sinfonia concertante in E flat, K. 364 (1779).

Piano concertos: No. 9 in E flat, K. 271 (1777); No. 12 in A, K. 414 (1782); No. 14 in E flat, K. 449 (1784); No. 15 in B flat, K. 450 (1784); No. 16 in D, K. 451 (1784); No. 17 in G, K. 453 (1784); No. 18 in B flat, K. 456 (1784); No. 19 in F, K. 459 (1784); No. 20 in D minor, K. 466 (1788); No. 21 in C, K. 467 (1785); No. 22 in E flat, K. 482 (1785); No. 23 in A, K. 488 (1786); No. 24 in C minor, K. 491 (1786); No. 25 in C, K. 503 (1786); No. 26 in D, K. 537 (1788) *Coronation*; No. 27 in B flat, K. 595 (1791); 2 pianos, in E flat, K. 365 (1779).

Other concertos: Violin – No. 3 in G, K. 216 (1775); No. 4 in D, K. 218 (1775) *Strasburg*; No. 5 in A, K. 219 (1775) *Turkish*; Adagio in E, K. 261 (1776). Bassoon – in B flat, K. 191 (1774). Clarinet – in A, K. 622 (1791). Flute – in G, K. 313 (1778); in D, K. 314 (1778) transcribed from oboe. Flute, harp in C, K. 299 (1778). Horn – No. 1 in D, K. 412 (1782); No. 2 in E flat, K. 417 (1783); No. 3 in E flat, K. 447 (1783); No. 4 in E flat, K. 495 (1786).

ORCHESTRAL MUSIC (continued)

Serenades: No. 6 in D, K. 239 (1776) *Notturna*; No. 7 in D, K. 250 (1776) *Haffner*; No. 9 in D, K. 320 (1779) *Posthorn*; No. 13 in G, K. 525 (1787) *Eine kleine Nachtmusik*. Wind instruments – No. 10 in B flat, K. 361 (1780) *Gran Partita*; No. 11 in E flat, K. 375 (1781); No. 12 in C minor, K. 388 (1782).

CHAMBER MUSIC

In this field Mozart also made an enormous contribution to the chamber music repertoire. It was not, however, his prime area of concern. The string quartets owe a great deal to Haydn, who was a source of inspiration for Mozart in quartet composition.

Quintets: Clarinet in A, K. 581 (1789). Strings – in C, K. 515 (1787); in G minor, K. 516 (1787); in D, K. 593 (1790); in E flat, K. 614 (1791).

Quartets: Flute – D major, K. 285 (1777). Oboe – F, K. 370 (1781). Strings – No. 11 in E flat, K. 171 (1773); No. 14 in G, K. 387 (1782); No. 15 in D minor, K. 421 (1783); No. 16 in E flat, K. 428 (1783); No. 17 in B flat, K. 458 (1784) *The Hunt*; No. 18 in A, K. 464 (1785); No. 19 in C, K. 465 (1785) *Dissonance*; Nos. 14 to 19 are the Haydn quartets. No. 20 in D, K. 499 (1786); No. 21 in D, K. 575 (1789); No. 22 in B flat, K. 589 (1790); No. 23 in F, K. 590 (1790); Nos. 21 to 23 are the Prussian quartets.

Trio: Divertimento in E flat, K. 563 (1788).

PIANO MUSIC

The piano was Mozart's own instrument, and he was taken on tour by his father as a child prodigy. Initially he was known in Vienna as a pianist, too. His knowledge of the instrument enabled him to write for it some of his most beautiful melodies as well as some of his most profound movements – especially in the piano concertos.

Quintet: Wind instruments – in E flat, K. 452 (1784).

Quartets: No. 1 in G minor, K. 478 (1785); No. 2 in E flat, K. 493 (1786).

Trios: No. 4 in E, K. 542 (1788); No. 6 in C, K. 564 (1788).

Sonatas: Violin and piano – No. 17 in C, K. 296 (1778); No. 26 in B flat, K. 378 (1781); No. 32 in B flat, K. 454 (1784); No. 34 in A, K. 526 (1787).

Piano solo: Sonatas – No. 4 in E flat, K. 282 (1775); No. 5 in G, K. 283 (1775); No. 8 in A minor, K. 310 (1778); No. 10 in C, K. 330 (1783); No. 11 in A. K. 331 (1783); No. 12 in F, K. 332 (1781–3); No. 14 in C minor, K. 457 (1784); No. 15 in C, K. 545 (1788); No. 17 in D, K. 576 (1789). Variations – in C, K. 265 on 'Ah, vous dirai-je, maman' (1778); in G, K. 455 on 'Unser dummer Pöbel meint' (1784). Fantasias – in C, K. 394 (1782); in D minor, K. 397 (1782). Rondos – in D, K. 485 (1786); in A minor, K. 511 (1787).

Glossary

Allegro An Italian word meaning cheerful, used to show that the music is to be played in a fast and lively way. It is also used for the name of a movement or section of a longer piece of music.

Andante An Italian word meaning going (in the sense of moving along) at a much slower pace than Allegro. Like Allegro, however, it is also used for the name of a movement.

Baroque Originally applied in architecture to whatever was strange, elaborate and ornate, but now used generally for courtly and aristocratic culture in general of the period from about 1600 to 1750.

Chamber music A type of music written for small groups of instruments. It was originally played in private rooms (chambers).

Concerto A piece of music in which a solo instrument, such as a violin, plays with an orchestra. A concerto usually has three movements.

Divertimento An Italian word meaning amusement or fun. Haydn used it to describe some of his string quartets, but Mozart used it for some of his instrumental works involving a number of movements.

Fantasia A musical composition that does not fall easily into any of the usual forms such as concerto, symphony or sonata with a set number of clearly defined movements or sections. At this period, often written for solo instrument.

Harmony The addition of notes to a melodic line or tune to produce a fuller, richer sound. When the addition of notes constitutes another melodic line then this becomes known as counterpoint.

Impresario The person who organises the hiring of artists and premises for recitals, concerts and operas – the latter a particularly complicated undertaking, with considerable financial risk, in the days before state funding for opera.

Libretto The text or words of an opera, set to music by a composer. The person who writes the text is called a librettist.

Mass The celebration of the Lord's Supper – Eucharist or Holy Communion – often set to music for voices with or without accompaniment. When the Mass is celebrated in memory of the dead, it is known as a Requiem.

Motet A composition for voices, usually for use in a church, but not a setting of words that are part of the liturgy or services – rather a comment on, or addition to, the liturgy.

Opera A play set to music for performance on the stage.

Patron A person who is willing to finance artists and their works. Most 18th-century composers and musicians depended on rich patrons for survival.

Psalm Usually one of the Psalms of David from the Bible, recited once a week in the Divine Office of the Catholic Church and once a month in the Anglican Church, though extracts are also appropriate to various feasts of the church year.

Quartet A group of four musicians. A string quartet consists of two violinists, one cellist and one viola player.

Quintet A group of five musicians, or piece of music for five instruments or voices. A string quintet consists of the same members as a quartet, with either an additional viola, cello or double bass. A piano quintet has a piano as the extra instrument.

Rondo A piece of music in which one section keeps returning from time to time, rather like a chorus or refrain.

Serenata A serenade, popular in the 18th century, often pastoral in character, and performed in the open air. It may be purely instrumental, but some kinds of cantata, or settings of words, are also called serenatas.

Singspiel A kind of opera developed in Germany and Austria in the 18th century. It is rather like a play with music and singing.

Sonata A piece of instrumental music, usually with three or four movements.

Symphony A piece of music written for full orchestra, usually with three or four movements.

Trio A group of three musicians. A string trio consists of a violinist, a cellist and a viola player.

Vespers The evening service of the western Church, on which the Evensong of the Anglican Church was based, with certain additions.

Viola The oldest member of the violin family, coming in size and tone between the violin and the cello. The *viola d'amore* has a set of sympathetic wire strings placed under the bowed strings and vibrating 'in sympathy' with them when they are played. This gives a silvery sheen to the sound of the instrument, which was favoured as a solo effect or in a chamber ensemble, rather than an orchestral one.

Index

Books to Read

Mozart by Eric Blom (Dent)
The Mozart Companion by D Mitchell and H C Robbins Landon (Faber)
Mozart by A Einstein (Granada)
Mozart: The Man. The Musician by Arthur Hutchings (Thames and Hudson)
The Life and Death of Mozart by Michael Levey (Weidenfeld)
Mozart the Young Musician by Nicholas Kenyon (Macdonald Educational)
Mozart by Kenneth and Valerie McLeish (Heinemann)
The Letters of Mozart and his Family by Emily Anderson (Macmillan)
Mozart by Henry Raynor (Macmillan)

Picture Research: Penny Warn and Tracy Rawlings

Photographs: Bildarchiv Preussicher Kulturbesitz 19 *top right*; The British Library 11 *centre*; The Fotomas Index 8, 11 *bottom*, 21 *bottom right*; Michael Holford 9 *top*, 13 *centre right*; Hunterian Art Gallery/University of Glasgow 18; The Mansell Collection 5, 10, 13 *top right*, 14, 15 *bottom*, 16, 23, 7 *top*; Internationale Stiftung Mozarteum/Salzburg 4 *inset*, 17 *top*, 19, 21 *bottom left*, 23 *top right*, 15 *top*, 23 *bottom right*; The Royal College of Music 13 *centre left*; Osterreichische Nationalbibliothek, Vienna 2–3, 21 *top left*; Salzburger Museum Carolino Augusteum 7 *bottom*, 17 *bottom*; Victoria and Albert Museum 9, Westermann Foto/H. Buresch 4, 11 *top*, 20, 21 *top right*, /Jack Skeel, Pluckley 12; 24–25 Westermann Foto/H. Buresch.